The Snowbira

How to live in sun year round.

Tracey Parnell
*Creativity***Guaranteed**.com
SnowBirdsofSarasota.ning.com

First Edition

Motivational Inspirational Self Help

2

Reviews

Tracey your book is a winner. It's real life!
Ron Klein
TheGrandfatherofPossibilities.com

This is a very fine book about the positives of being a Snowbird like Tracey is. If you know her, buy it and gift it to a Northerner!
Doug Ross, Ph.D.

*Creativity*Guaranteed.com

Publisher, Self Published (email me for source)
Copyright © 2009 by Tracey Parnell, CreativityGuaranteed.com.
Producer, Writer and Author, Tracey Parnell
Early Readers Edition – January 1, 2010 (100 copies)
First Edition to be published February 14, 2010
Note to writers: If you are planning on quoting any portion of this
book contents in a review, please cross reference any quotation
using the First Edition February 14, 2010 version. Thank you

*Creativity***Guaranteed**.com

This book is dedicated to Dena and Ken Parnell. Their love and support provide me with constant pride, comfort and security.

Dreams are only realized when one takes action. They both taught me how to dream. They also inspired me to make my dreams come true no matter what.

CONTENTS

10 chapters to Becoming a Snowbird

*Creativity*Guaranteed.com

Dedicated to Buster and Bugsy 2010

Introduction

When you are finished reading this book you will have the knowledge, resources and proof that you too can spend your winters snow free and south of the border. I have spent my past twelve years living where I choose to live, without the aid of simple answers or resources. The lifestyle I created was not handed to me either. I simply made the decision to do it and took action! With determination and perseverance, eventually, it all fell into place. Changing the quality of my thoughts had to be one of the main tools that helped me succeed.

Review

"EXCELLENT BOOK CHOCK FILLED WITH VALUABLE HINTS AND INFORMATION"...Charles M. Bonasera

*Creativity*Guaranteed.com

What is in it for you? This is a very good question.

- A 364 day sunny summer (one day it rains)
- A snowless winter
- Live like a movie star (no talent required)
- No more shoveling snow and driving on icy roads
- Affordable Living (maybe even save some money along the way)
- Avoid costly mistakes
- Get unstuck
- Maybe, meet the person of your dreams or a life partner
- Double your friendship or business customer base
- My personal promise to answer your questions via email

I wrote this book to share my secret. I now live in paradise 364 days of the year. I have created a lifestyle that I know with certainty has increased my life span by 10–20 years. I wish to share with you my perspective and strategies, so you and yours may accomplish the same.

CreativityGuaranteed.com

About the Author

I became a snowbird at the age of 32 and have spent the past 10 winters in Florida. I decided to live the life as a snowbird mainly because of the harsh winters of my homeland, Canada. Although I remain a proud Canadian citizen, I choose to spend the winter months in Florida. I get to experience the best both worlds have to offer. Professionally, I am an artist and an entrepreneur. I am the founder of *Creativity*Guaranteed.com a creative career management company. I also paint, invent and create every day. My economic lifestyle, health and overall well being have increased dramatically by choosing to live where I desire year round. I am eager to share my secrets of how you can live where you desire. With a can-do attitude and a purposeful plan there is nothing you cannot create for yourself. GUARANTEED!

Legal Notice
The author has attempted to be as accurate as possible in the development of this book. The information should be considered time sensitive and that through the natural evolution of time, market conditions will also shift and change. It should be noted that what may have worked in

previous decades or times may not be applicable today.

The author is not responsible for any outcome of 3rd party events, promoters or speakers representing this book without permission. In attempt to assist each reader in achieving your goals, the author has offered personal one time advice to any person or organization that has purchased this book.

Send your questions and comments to Tracey@CreativityGuaranteed.com and allow 72 hours for a response.

This book is not intended for the use of legal accounting or financial advice. This book was created in 12-point font for reader ease. If you have, comments or suggestions send via email. Tracey@CreativityGuaranteed.com

FOREWORD by Charles M. Bonasera

I met Tracey for the first time at a Y.E.S. networking group meeting in Sarasota, Florida. The group's members are all entrepreneurs in a vast number of different marketing areas attempting to learn from and support one another in their endeavors. This day, she was to present the "Entrepreneur of the Week". Although somewhat anxious previous to her presentation, once she started to speak, her natural ability, passion, drive and successful career shone through.

She spoke of her beloved father whom she considered her model and mentor as being a true entrepreneur who was many years ahead of his time in his business risks and accomplishments. She spoke not only of those accomplishments but of the deep-seated emotions and love that she has for him. A few times, I looked around the room as she spoke and the audience was mesmerized. I, too, was deeply touched and impressed with her and her presentation. She continually spoke of his "passion" as well as her own as being the key to success in life and in business as well.

I had just recently come away from a very poor business experience and was on the verge of "hanging it up" in terms of continuing in my second career of being a life and business consultant, author and motivational speaker. Instead, I gravitated toward her at the end of the meeting as did several other audience participants, not only to congratulate her on her fine presentation but to ask her opinion as to whether continuing was feasible after I gave her a brief synopsis of my business experience in Florida. She gave me her full attention, listened intently to my spiel with understanding and then simply said "let's talk" upon which she handed me her business card with the title "Creativity Guaranteed".

Needless to say, I became one of her valued clients and, ultimately, I consider her to be a very close and dear friend. To extol Tracey's virtues would take a book in and of itself. She is one of the most passionate persons about what she does that I have ever met and I had met hundreds of them in my professional career which spanned many years. She is warm yet discerning. Her intelligence is only surpassed by her dedication to helping every person find their niche both in life and in business. Her positive approach to the most complex, knotty and seemingly irresolvable issues contains methodical, down-to-earth and easy to follow steps that help her clients to achieve their purpose in consulting with her.

Her vast experience in the business world and the practical solutions that she offers from lessons learned in her own life are truly remarkable. I have talked with many of her clients and have never heard anything but high praise for her abilities and approach to problem-solving. It is both my personal and professional opinion that this young lady is truly blessed and that she shares those blessings with anyone and everyone she encounters … whether they become a client of hers or not.

I am thankful for having been at that first meeting and look forward to many more with Tracey Parnell. I would strongly advise everyone reading this book to read it carefully and then re-read it since it contains many of the "secrets of life" that we all seek. Her wisdom transcends her forty two years of life. Just one more comment. Tracey's work with people is all about changing their lifestyles in order to realize their passion in life … no matter what it may be and when in life they choose to accomplish it. She "practices what she preaches" in that she has created a lifestyle for herself that most people would wait to accomplish

16

until retirement. Whatever a person's challenge …
whatever their dream of a different lifestyle …
Tracey will help them to realize it by using the
secrets and methods that she employs in dealing
with her own life.

Charles M. Bonasera, LCSW,
Consultant, Author, Ghost Writer and Motivational
Speaker   www.CharlesMBonasera.com

Chapter 1

Become a Snowbird and live where you desire year round.

This chapter is dedicated to my father, teacher and friend
Ken Parnell.
Ken has taught me the importance of integrity, honesty and
compassion.

Words to live by: "Don't tell me, Show me." - Ken Parnell

When I became a Snowbird and decided to live in Florida for my winters, I became a different and some would say, new person. I no longer dreaded the coming of winters in Canada. I would embrace the cool weather of a Canadian fall season with a smile. I knew in only a matter of weeks I would be on a warm sunny beach. Imagine with me for a moment never having to see or shovel snow again. Never again would you have to navigate your car through black ice, sleet and freezing rain.

I made the decision to become a snowbird at age 32 and never looked back. Once I made the transition, I seriously could not figure out why everyone was not living this lifestyle. Yes, it seemed too good to be true. I have often said to my Canadian friends and family, "*I wish I could send the sun to you*", but until then, we must chase the sun and relocate to experience paradise year round. In these times especially, given environmental weather changes alone, relocating is becoming a predominant reality. Our current economy coupled with our evolving political situation will force us to challenge our geographic choices at one point or another.

The good news is I know and believe there is enough room on this planet for all of us to live where we truly desire to live year round. The question is - are you living where you want to live year round? If not, is your reason good enough to prevent you from living your dreams? Really, this is an important question to ask oneself. It is important you know what is blocking you from living where you want to live. I emphasize this point because I spent ten years telling myself all the reasons why I could not possibly leave my country. As a result I robbed myself of the joy one experiences when you get to live in paradise year round. I ask my clients and friends often, why don't you just take the plunge and relocate? The answers I receive, although valid and true are really nothing more than temporary roadblocks. They may say: my job, my wife, my husband, my kids my, my, my…

The truth is if you are not living the life you truly desire or *where* you desire, it is usually because of one of these reasons:

1. You may be stuck in fear or self-doubt *or both.*
2. You are resisting "change".
3. You may be simply asking yourself the WRONG questions and/or;
4. You may simply not know WHAT you want.

Whatever the reason, there is hope and please know that it can be resolved by the time you finish reading this book. Reinventing your life to live where you want to live year round becomes easier if you consider adopting two important ideas.

1. Get comfortable with change.
2. Become willing to do what it takes for change.

These are two very simple statements. You are ready for change or you are not. If you are ready and willing get comfortable and allow me to introduce you some neat ideas.

Life is too short to be spending the majority of time where you are not happy, content and inspired. I spent my first 32 winter years in Canada. Driving on ice, freezing my fingers to the

21

bone and going months without feeling the warmth of the sun, became my way of life. Having my car's heater kick in just as I arrived to work was a particular pet peeve. Snow and ice are for some, but not for me! Do not get me wrong, I love my homeland Canada. The thing is…I love it from May to October.

I say this now to encourage you to embrace any misery or frustration you may currently have. Discontentment is the first step in change.

My years working with celebrities and professional athletes also inspired me to live where I was happy year round. I discovered living in paradise is not just for the rich and famous. There are key ingredients most celebrities know about but often do not speak of. One of the keys is ABUNDANCE. Having the knowledge there is Abundance everywhere you go. Another key is to decide where you wish to live and simply take action. Once you are in your desired location you then can recreate your life as you wish. The main lesson here I learned was anyone can make a living just about anywhere. I also would copy the tactics used by my funny comedic friends like Carla Collins, Michael Lamport and Tonya Lee Williams.

Find someone who has done what you wish to do and ask them how they did it. Trust me they will tell you.

Another key to my success is I learned to incorporate the advice of my father who often says *"use your brain, not your back"* to make money. What expertise do you have that you could offer others? Guaranteed someone seeks the knowledge you already have and is willing to pay for it.

During the winters in Canada, at times, I would become isolated. I would choose not to leave my cozy home unless I absolutely had to brave the cold. Sadness and even depression can set in when we rob ourselves of being outdoors or worse rob ourselves of the life each and every one of us desires and deserves. We all deserve to live where we want to live year round. In these current times there is not one reason we cannot live where we want to live year round.

I have spent the last ten winters in sunny, warm Florida. I now have a 364 day summer – one day it rains. In a nutshell, I simply choose my desired location and then figured out the logistics. It is a simple matter of choice.

I had a job, relationships and other things I could have used as excuses to stay put. For ten years, I did just that. "I cannot possibly move to Florida" is what I thought, said and believed and guess what, I got exactly what I thought, said and believed.

Next time you hear yourself say "I can't", stop for a moment and think but what if I could?

It was not until I changed my way of thinking, changed the quality of my questions and took a chance did I find the way to live the life I live today. I created a life of passion and purpose and you can do the same. It matters not what your financial circumstances are, your family life or what your current job is. What matters is "what is going on between your ears". What do you think, say and believe? Chances are whatever your answer is, you are getting just that.

One of the most inspiring and life defining moments I have had is when I saw Christopher Reeves move his baby finger. You remember Superman right? After years of being completely paralyzed from the neck down he sat on stage in his wheelchair and moved his pinky finger to denote the message "never give up dreaming".

At that very moment, I decided that no excuse is good enough anymore.

Getting what you want can be created by first *identifying* WHAT you want.

On my way to work each winter day in Canada I would turn my face to the sun through my car window and say "how sweet life would be if I had the sun on my face each day". I knew I was not content living my winters in the snow but I could not see any way out. We tend to do what we have been programmed to do. Who is currently programming your life? It is when you decide to take charge and live your passion and purpose that you will find personal joy and contentment. Part of my passion statement is living a healthy life in a warm climate.

Where have you always desired to live?

Living the life of a snowbird does not necessarily mean you have to spend your winters in Florida or somewhere south of the border. Living where you want when you want could mean you are a Floridian and wish to get out of the heat during the summers. Take the test. Are you living where you want to live 365 days of the year?

If not, then consider spending your year divided into two places. This way you will need to have two locations to call your home which means double the expense – or does it?

One year I spent the majority of my winter in a hotel. Most people would immediately exclaim - *How expensive and impractical is that*? Well, I made it very affordable and it was due to my approach and by asking creative questions. I asked the hotel owner if I rented a room for 30 days what room rate could he offer. He began by saying, "$70 a night". Then I asked if I paid it all up front would that be helpful to him? He answered "Yes". Then I asked what if I were to not need daily housekeeping and only require it once a week? Would that be helpful in reducing your overhead costs, I asked? He answered, "Yes". I could see his interest level rise as I continued to suggest ways I could help him as a business owner.

I then offered to physically move each day to any unused or unsold hotel room. Every hotel ends up with some unoccupied rooms each day. That is just a natural fact of the hotel business. Essentially I would be staying in a room that otherwise would have gone empty due to no particular demand on that given day. That did not

26

inconvenience me in the least because I was living out of a suitcase anyway. In fact, on several occasions I ended up in the $250-a-night penthouse. Now can you see why I am a strong advocator to *"Think outside the box".*

I simply thought, what is the difference or inconvenience to have to simply move up or down the hallway or a floor? When you are literally 20 steps to the clear sandy warm beach those silly logistics seem to matter less and less.

As I asked my questions, the starting price of $70 a night was eventually reduced and we settled on $40 a night. We both created a win-win situation. I had budgeted that year to stay one month in that city. Because of my creative approach, I stayed three months and did not compromise my budget in any way.

Ask, how can this be created?
Ask, what if this could be created?
What is your little dream you have tucked away?
What if it were possible?

Winter is for the dogs
MayDay Burnside

*Creativity*Guaranteed.com

Chapter 2

Tap into Your Passion

This chapter is dedicated to my mother who has provided me with abundant creativity.
She was the first person to show me how to live a life of passion and compassion.
She also provides unconditional encouragement to embrace my talents.
Words to live by: "Everyone has the ability to do anything, they set their mind to" - Dena Parnell

Passion

What is your Passion? If you are going to start from scratch and move to a place you always wanted to live why not incorporate into the equation – your passion? Living a more fulfilling life is not only about geography it is about fulfilling your dreams and doing what makes you happy.

If you are not living your passion and purpose every day it is probably because of one or more of the following reasons:

- You don't know what your passion is or what will make you happy?
- You believe "*it is too late*"
- You are fearful of … whatever - it may be…

That is not bad news. It is actually quite the opposite. If you identify with any of the above mentioned limitations, good! Everyone I know personally that is living a life of purpose and passion had to start exactly at that point. Maybe you are at that point now. If that is your case, I have three great suggestions to help you find your passion(s).

Kindergarden Question

Answer this question: What did you do when you were in kindergarden?
When we were in kindergarden we gravitated to the things that gave us the most pleasure. We were at an age when peer pressure, financial constraints and self-sabotage were not present.

Personally when I think back to that time, both of my hands were covered in paint as I smeared paint on a large sheet of art paper attempting to create art. I was in my natural, untouched state of bliss. I was allowed to be messy. I did not have to follow any rules and there were no such concerns as judgment, time or money. Today, part of my business and income is derived from my artwork. I have sold over 100 paintings and have my art showcased in various locations. A greeting card line also supports my multiple

30

streams of income strategy. The greeting cards showcase my art images and photography. I learned that income strategy from my mentor, John Greer.

Getting in touch with your inner child will help define or refine a passion you may have forgotten about. You can go to the following address on the internet to view my creations, inventions and artwork: www.creativityguaranteed.com/my_art.

What is your creative outlet?

If you are planning on working in another country you must adhere to the laws and obtain proper documents and permits. Contact the Internal Revenue Service (IRS) in your country of origin for your rights and working options. There are several options you may not have considered that may be available to you.

I have designed a company and income around my lifestyle and no one person out there is incapable of doing what I have done. My goal was to be paid to be creative every day. Now I can confidently say that I am paid to be creative every day.

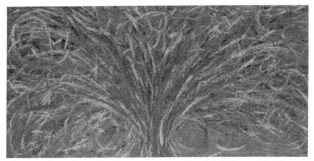

Painting by self-taught artist Tracey Parnell,
CreativityGuaranteed.com
Photography by Tracey Parnell, artwork currently residing with
Josh Odea

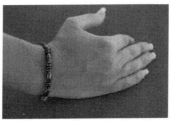

"Creating magnetic bracelets is another one of my creative outlets"
The magnets have been proven to offer relief for those suffering
with pain.
"When I create, life is good!" Tracey Parnell.
Model is Sandra Valente, Photography by Tracey Parnell

Zero Day Challenge – Finding your Passion

I have magically granted you an eighth day in this coming week. We are going to call it a zero day. This zero day does not count, there is no such thing as work or family or anything for that matter. It is a mysterious day that you can take whenever you muster the fortitude to block off an entire day from that chunk of time we refer to as life. Take your day planner and actually mark it or cross off the day as "Zero Day". Book nothing, allow no appointments to be scheduled and tell no one you are doing that. And presto, you have one complete day free from appointments, duties or chores.

Your challenge should you wish to take it, is to do absolutely *nothing:* simply exist for this Zero day. Do what you feel like doing all day long, do nothing, do everything: the only rule is *Do not schedule anything.* Allow your day to be 100% clear of the regular appointments and must do's. Allow the day to unfold naturally and see what happens. If you can book a day and do just what I described, you will not only tap into your passion clues you will also discover much about yourself. Contact me via email for some further suggestions if you have no success.

Fast Track - Quick Tips and Hints *to Finding Your Passion*

Answer the following questions:
I lose track of time when I …
If I were a millionaire, I would spend my time…
On my last vacation, I had the most fun when I…

I must stress that it matters not what your passion is: it simply matters that you identify your passion and start living it. Do not feel limited to one. Go ahead and pick two, three, or four. I have been able to incorporate sailing, painting, and my love of dogs into my business on a daily basis. I am paid to live my passion and purpose every day. What would you love to do every day?

Acrylic painting by Robert E. Foster, CreativityGuaranteed.com
Robert is a self-taught painter who began to paint at age 50.

My mother loves to create. She spends countless hours creating the most beautiful blankets, scarves, mittens and hats. She simply does it because she loves to do it. She could develop this love and passion into a business and make a respectable amount of money but she chooses not to. Instead she chooses to donate her creations to countless hospitals, churches, and homeless shelters. The world is a better place because of people like my mother.

A wonderful part of finding your passion and purpose is you make up the rules as you go. There is no government or boss to tell you differently. The key is to find your passion and purpose and find a way to live them each day. There are examples of people living their passion and purpose everywhere if you simply seek them out. Can't you tell instantly when you meet someone who loves his or her job? I know we can all relate to meeting people who clearly do not love their job. You can find them abundantly at banks, crossing borders, and fast-food restaurants. When you tap into your passion and find a way to make money from it, there is no limit to your income potential. You wake up thinking about it and go to sleep thinking about it.

Starting a small business is one of the quickest ways to create a job for yourself, particularly when you live abroad. Small businesses can be seasonal, mobile and best of all can be based on your passion. I recommend to all my clients to start a small business at some point in their lives. It matters not what income you strive for it matters that you took the risk and started something you believed in. It matters that you had the opportunity to live out your passion and purpose.

I started with a simple truth and strength about myself. I am creative. I created my mission statement. "I get paid to be creative every day"

My father always said, "Don't tell me, show me". The following is a number of ways I get paid to be creative every day in my businesses.

I get paid to:

Paint abstract artwork
Shoot weddings as a photographer
Organize Businesses
Teach time Management
Send Greeting Cards online
Shop at home
Dog walk/sit

Photography by Tracey Parnell

Organize and coach business leaders
Inspire others by leading *my* perfect life
Teach yoga
Co-create businesses for my clients
Problem solve for businesses
Brainstorm with struggling business owners
Walk the beach with clients
Coach celebrities through auditions
Help authors rid writers block
Mind map with clients considering new career paths
Write everyday whatever I want to write about
Learn new skills everyday
Play with puppies at least once a week
Inspire people to greater heights
Coach artists to get paid to be creative

37

*Creativity*Guaranteed.com

Share my knowledge with my employees
Invest in small businesses
Teach Event Planning Certification Programs
Teach Meeting Planning Certification Programs
Design Graphics
Deliver speeches
Design floor plans
Certify event planners
Co-create exit strategies
Help struggling artists get recognition
Create and design jewelry
Co-create career strategies
Raise funds for the less fortunate
Advisory Board Member
Rescue and save animals at risk
Train people to become effective public speakers
Coach executives to reorganize their companies
Visit the sick and less fortunate

Jack, after a day of work, is exhausted,
but still willing to go back if necessary.

*100% of any income derived from animal rescue/services/therapy
benefits The Humane Society of Sarasota, Florida.*

*Creativity***Guaranteed**.com

Buster gets a baby of his very own.
Photographer Carla Collins & Tyrone Power Jr.

Bugsy loves his whole family.

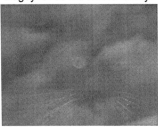

Model Maggie-Mae discovers
Terri Swope, Famous Photographer in the making

39

Best of all, I get paid every day to be creative. What would you really like to do with your time if money was not a factor? Whatever your list looks like, trust me that it can be turned into a business. You may have to start several businesses to fulfill all your passions but I only see that as a plus. I personally have several business ventures I am involved with. Life is definitely more fascinating when you have your hand in several projects.

A fine example of a small business owner incorporating passion is a friend of mine that combined his wife's love for cooking with his love of dogs. They run and operate a dog cookie company in Florida.

What is your hobby?
_____

Do you believe someone is willing to pay you to play?
YES / NO

Want Proof?
Anyone who knows me personally knows one of my passions is my dogs. I care for up to 33 dogs all over the world.
These special dogs know me as Aunt Tracey.

I could have made my services available as part of my business and charge a fee however I choose instead to do something rather creative. I ask the owner of whatever dog I am caring for to consider donating to the Humane Society of their chosen city. This way we generate funding for the Humane Society, they receive a tax receipt and I get much appreciated time with one of my dogs. Living your life as you choose does not always have to do with money. My company has raised over three million dollars to date for not-for-profit organizations worldwide.

Our newest sweetest additions: Isabella and Ivan.
Photography by Tenille Dixon, Mary Kay Consultant

Can you turn your hobby into a revenue stream? I beg of you, believe me now when I say, Yes you can!

CreativityGuaranteed.com

Okay, maybe you still do not believe me. Allow me then to prove that there are customers willing to pay you to play. Let me prove it. Start a business and send me your product and or service offer. I will be your first customer. The only catch is that you must be living where you desire 364 days of the year. Part of my purpose in life is to inspire others to live a life of passion and purpose. So I dare you to go ahead and discover your passion. Then simply find a way to get paid to do it.

Live your passion
Discover your purpose
Live where you choose to live 365 days of the year

Easy to say
Easy to understand
Challenging, but not impossible to do

It's Too Late or is it?

One of my dearest friends Leonora Girgenti is one fine example of someone living out her passions and purpose. When I first met Leonora she was working in a grey, cold, stark building on the 22nd floor as a corporate trainer. I met her in her beautifully decorated one-of-a-kind office. She had arranged with the maintenance manager for the control of the lighting intensity so she could install more home-like atmospheric lighting fixtures.

Her choice in artwork was full of color, class and life. She even somehow made her office smell like lavender and roses, I recall. I asked her, "Why is your office so different from the rest and so beautifully designed and decorated?" She replied, "I like to be around beauty and I love to design." Now here was a perfect example of someone that was not getting paid to do what she loved most: decorating and creating. In a period of one year Leonora changed that. She attracted not only a career whereby she could design and create all day but in the process met the man of her dreams. Leonora lives in Canada in her personally self-designed and built beautiful house with the man of her dreams Stefano, and their two children, Charles and Isabella.

Another friend of mine Sandy Norton creates T-shirts from one simple word that inspires her. The word is *everyday* and it inspired an entire company. Her inspirational clothing offers words like Sunshine, Breathe and Celebrate. She then added on the word "everyday" below each inspiring word. *Sunshine***Everyday**.com is a popular T-shirt line that sells to the masses worldwide. Sandy is a fine example of doing what you love to do. When I asked Sandy why she loves making T-shirts she said "It makes me smile and the world needs them." I can't think of a better example of making a business based on your passion and purpose.

Big Red "The best theft in town"

I incorporate dogs into my daily work. Why, because one of my passions are my dogs.

Chapter 3

Discover Your *Purpose*

This chapter is dedicated to my partner Robert.
Bob has provided me with the courage to stand alone, but I have
the inspiration and desire to stand by his side.
Having a partner that supports me unconditionally is a great honor.

Why were you put on this planet?

If you do not have a solid and sound answer to that question please read this section carefully. Part of my purpose in life is to help others find their passion and purpose. Nothing bothers me more than to see people roaming this planet lacking purpose and in pain. Some just go through the motions with very little or simply no happiness in their lives. That is just *not* necessary when there are infinite amounts of happiness for everyone.

It is my belief that those who are living a purposeful life will not only stay on this planet longer, but will experience joy and happiness every day. When we tap into our purpose and

*Creativity*Guaranteed.com

live it each day, our world changes into a place of wonderment and abundance.

Isn't life too short to be living where you struggle to survive? Where would you live if you could? How about Australia, Italy or Costa Rica?

I believe our life experience is intended to be meaningful and purposeful. What does this have to do with being a snowbird you may ask? Living a life you have personally designed and created not only includes your geographic location but really so much more.

Once you reinvent your life, to live where you wish to live, you will thirst for more. Improvements, upgrades and enhancements to your quality of life will become eminent. You will have created the environment in which you are most comfortable. Your spirit is ready to soar. You are no longer consumed by the discomfort of living in a location that is not natural or comfortable to you. Remove this huge obstacle and a space is created for lifestyle enhancements. Most people I have encountered that live where they wish to live begin to ask questions about how to find more happiness and improve their overall quality of life. They eventually ask how they can serve others or how they can contribute to leaving a better world.

46

Let us say, I gave you one million dollars free and clear. Now pretend for a moment you believed me, come on, just try.

Would this gesture make you smile? What if I told you, you may have the one million dollars but you must live in Alaska for the winter months? Now if you were perhaps a penguin or someone who loves the snow that proposal would appeal to you. However, the majority of us, I would venture to guess, would rather take the million and plant ourselves in a sunny spot under a beach umbrella. If you lived where you wanted to live 364 days of the year, would you be happier and more content?

Living for today or living in the present is *one of my keys* to happiness. If you can do that and begin to truly appreciate each day you may begin to then ask "*Why am I here*"? Living our purpose each day is something we all would become more content with if we could live it. Simply identify your purpose and create a purpose statement.

Here are some of the most common objections, excuses or arguments that I hear from others when they neglect to create a powerful purpose statement.

47

I do not have a purpose statement because:

- I can't pick just one purpose.
- It's too late to live my purpose.
- I have no idea what my purpose is - where would I even start?

When I hear those objections, my response is, Great, now we know where to start. The two important parts of finding your purpose are willingness & attitude.

If you seek the answer with an open mind and if you trust the process you will find and know your purpose by the end of this chapter. Decide for yourself what feels the best for you at this point in time. Either way, I hope to see you on the beach one day when and if you are ready.

Here are some questions to ask about establishing your purpose. Pretend with me for a moment, will you? Let us look into the future say 50 years or so. Now envision yourself comfortably sitting in a rocking chair. Consider how you would complete these statements.

My life was worthwhile because_____

My most enjoyable experience
was_____

The best part of my family life
was_____

I helped_____

The most remarkable trip I took
was_____

Once you have completed that section you should have some "clues" into your purpose. Finding your purpose is not like turning on a light bulb. *Presto here it is*, although I have seen that happen. Finding your purpose is much like looking at a painting or picture. Sometimes it comes to you as the complete painting and other times it comes in the form of puzzle pieces. If you are collecting pieces or clues, keep doing so. Soon you will have enough pieces to fit together into a complete painting or picture.

I suggest you keep a log or checklist going called, "My Purpose*"* and add to it as you discover clues along the way.

A living hero of mine is a man named Mickey Choothesa. Mickey is a traveling photographer who is living his passion and purpose. Mickey became a diplomat and fundraiser in the interest of protecting children worldwide. His love of adventure, photography and the protection of children's rights were melded into a career that can only be described as a career *of passion and purpose*. If you want to transport yourself around the world viewing gorgeous images, check out Mickey's site.

www.MickeyChoothesa.com

Another key thing to remember is to not overthink this exercise, keeping it simple.

Mother Theresa's purpose was
to help people avoid suffering

Martin Luther King had a dream

Identify your purpose, not just any purpose, create one that will allow you to fully live a purposeful life.

Surround Yourself with Successful, Balanced and Passionate People.

What does your purpose have to do with being a snowbird? Becoming a snowbird can be all about

50

becoming happier and more content. Once you have the geography figured out purpose quickly follows. I am confident that if you are seeking knowledge to become a snowbird, you are already 90% there. It may not feel like it from where you sit but I beg of you to continue and focus on taking one step at a time.

In this book, I offer these lessons about purpose to give you a quicker way to personal fulfillment.

What you focus on is what you get!

It can be that simple!

What are you focused on right now?

I blocked out the focus exercise for years because I simply felt too much *self-imposed* pressure.

Consider the following approach.

Pretend for a moment that you are in the great-grandmother or great-grandfather stage of your life. Fill in the blanks if you wish.

I learned that the key to happiness was

_____

The key to my physical well-being was_____

I was known as a professional
_____

My friends and family were_____

My favorite housing experience was when I lived_____

My contribution to leaving a better planet was_____

My money is ever flowing now, because I
_____

My chosen most favorite location to live was_____

Nothing yet? Try the following.

Volunteer/Fundraise/Give Back

Volunteering at a hospital, Humane Society or non-profit group is an easy way to meet people and a wonderful use of your time. Just think-if not one person ever considered giving back to the community-where would we be?

We all have in common one thing. We are all trying to avoid suffering and we are trying to find happiness. Finding happiness has much to do with finding your passion and purpose. Your purpose can be simple to discover when you ask the right questions. If you cannot come up with the questions, serving others is a sure fire way to get your answers.

BigRed Burnside

Getting What You Want!

Consider articulating what you want into a 30-second elevator speech. An elevator speech is nothing more than three to five sentences you can recite that will inform the listener with exactly what it is you are seeking.

Next, recite your speech to as many people as possible. Do not be shy or rule anyone out. Tell your butcher, tell your wife, tell anyone who will listen. There is a 90% chance you already know the person with the answer to your every question, concern or desire. They cannot give you the solution until they know your question. That is a particularity excellent technique when seeking a job, mate or anything else for that matter.

Get what you want *Extraordinaire*
John Greer, co-creator YES941.com
A mentor and dear friend

54

Chapter 4

Accommodations

Dedicated to
Charles M. Bonasera
Wisdom is the best word I can use when describing Charles.
Charles most endearing quality is his fearlessness when it comes
to asking questions.
Charles and his wife are happily living in Florida after his 40-year
successful practice as a psychotherapist.
Words to live by: "This too shall pass" - Charles Bonasera

For an extended amount of time, go to where you wish to live. Ask and interview everyone you come in contact with about housing, transportation and accommodations.

Did you know there are many houses in Florida just sitting vacant? The housing industry has taken a downward turn and the resale housing market is painfully slow. Now this too shall pass with time. My point here is to find out what is going on economically with respect to housing in the city where you want to move. Regardless of the housing market conditions there is ample opportunity everywhere when you simply investigate. Investigation is nothing more than asking questions and sometimes role-playing.

Read the local newspapers and magazines.

Tourist and Welcome Centers are one of the quickest ways to find out what is happening in the city. I make it a habit to go into the welcome center of the city I am visiting and say "I may be moving to this city next month". What can you tell me about housing options?" You have nothing to lose and everything to gain. The key to finding affordable housing is your mindset and the quality of your questions. Instead of thinking like a vacationer or tourist, think like you are already a resident. That simple difference will save you a lot of time and money.

Another great tip is to go to the mom and pop shops for breakfast or when you go shopping. Those shops are run by the local people and they can tell you what is really going on in the city. Again, you must ask the right questions.

Selecting a Location

If you already know what city you prefer then you want to sort through travel options and living accommodations.

It is interesting to me to explore all the options when considering housing. Most people do not know about the alternatives that are available. I want to tell a short story about a new friend I made recently. Brenda Eilers runs her own business in Florida called ITEX www.The-Barter-Company.com. Brenda is in her thirties and owns 19 homes. It was all possible through ITEX, which allows you to buy and sell virtually anything including homes on a barter system. That means you could become a member and "trade out," so to speak, your services. You offer your services and build up credits and you can then pay your rent and/or mortgage in ITEX dollars. That is a smart strategy to keep your cash output to a minimum. That is an example of a brilliant and creative solution to housing. It is also an example to being open to learning anything and everything out there. Once you know all your options, another new invention is being created, so never stop asking others for solutions.

There are several barter companies offering similar services. Research them all to find the right one for your circumstances and situation.

Many trade arrangements can be made informally as well between your existing friends and clients.

Need furniture? Try www.FREEcycle.org.

Accommodations

Another accommodation alternative is for you to find a roommate or couple willing to split the rent. Personal ads often reveal wealthy homeowners who choose to rent out their mansion for the seasonal months such as, January, February and March. They then can use the money for their own desired travel plans. In one case, the three-month seasonal income the homeowner received was equivalent to an entire year's mortgage payment. Even the rich can be very cleaver and seem to never stop finding ways to make/save money.

Spread the word and tell everyone who is willing to listen what you are seeking.
Never tire of communicating exactly what it is in full detail. Consider some non-traditional housing options.

Live on a boat
Find a roommate to share your costs
House swap (international options)
Research extended stay at meditation resorts
Travel and stay in monasteries
Become a nanny
Offer your services in trade for rent
Investigate student exchange programs

One of my hideaways on the water

Did you ever think of driving and living in a recreational vehicle?

Research some helpful RV websites:
- RV Free Classifieds
- RV chat rooms or blogs to connect with other travelers
- Great outdoor companies
- Go Camping America
- Go Camping Canada

NHTSA - National Highway Traffic Safety Administration lists all camping sites.
North American Truck Camper Owners Association also offers much good advice.

Rent in a number of locations prior to purchasing property or settling down for a long period. That will give you a better sense of the area and more about the local culture and atmosphere.

The snowbird lifestyle can be active and exciting. And the less you spend on accommodations, the more you can afford to extend your stay. Affordable accommodations are extremely important. My personal desire is to request and ensure that my accommodations are safe and clean. When you spend the majority of your time on the beach your traditional accommodations minimum standards mysteriously can be negotiated.

Contact local public offices, such as the tourist board or chamber of commerce for social and housing resources. The municipal economic development office can be a source of information on local issues such as housing, taxes and services.

Time Shares

Be very cautious and research all the conditions before signing on the dotted line. For some, this solution can be very effective and pleasant however, I would proceed with extreme caution. Blackout dates, clauses, and conditions of the time share company can be particular areas of contention.

Buying a House or Condo

Be aware of the county taxes because each state varies dramatically. Being a U.S. citizen, has many lower-tax options for homeowners. If you are technically a snowbird and not a U.S. citizen your taxes may and most likely will be higher. www.Zillow.com is a great resource for determining property value, from which you can determine your property tax estimate.

Communications

Telephone communications can be a challenge when living in two locations. Research your communications options in your desired new location by calling all the local providers. Ask other residents what options they are using. There is no easy answer out there. Most systems are not designed to support snowbirds and, in fact, they can seem to be not only neglectful and unfair but defiant as well. I found the most effective way to address communications is to ask 10 people around you what they are using and paying. The chances are that you will be able to come up with your own customized way to satisfy any communications need and desire you have. "No contract" cellular phones and Skype are excellent communication tools.

When you are physically not present in one of your homes, offer a recording on your messaging services that gives your alternative number but never say you are out of the country. That can be an invitation to burglars and such. Simply tell close family and friends about your extended travel plans. For safety reasons tell them where and when you expect to be and then be considerate and follow through with a call of courtesy upon your arrival.

You GOT Mail

Having mail forwarded is a popular option. You can also get a PO mailbox for a short time. Mail, flyers, and newspapers to your Canadian or other main place of residence should not be overlooked since piled up mail is a green light for burglars.

*Creativity*Guaranteed.com

Email

Email account is almost a necessity these days. Yahoo and Hotmail offer free addresses and can be obtained with the click of about 3 steps.

Home Watch

If you cannot get someone to watch and take care of your house hire a professional service. An entrepreneurial friend informed me that the insurance companies insist you have your home inspected while away on extended vacations every three days. Come on, every three days? Simply call your insurance company, inquire, and of course read your policy about extended vacations. There are companies you can hire such as www.LifesaTrip.ca that offers property watch services. I like to ask a trusted friend to perform this duty.

Toll Free 888-862-7978
www.LifesaTrip.ca

Wherever you end up, think through your communication needs. Will you have a landline, use cellular or VOIP (Voice-Over-Internet-Protocol) or Skype.

Whatever you choose, call the company you are going to use and get the full pricing and conditions. I once saw an $800 cell phone bill for one month because the person did not know or understand roaming charges.

Even Puppies need and seek purpose.
Hire your dog, give him/her a purpose.
They will become more fulfilled and happy.

64

Chapter 5

Retired? Now What?

Dedicated to Sam Swope
Sam is a talented person who is living life as a snowbird between
Florida and his northern home.
Sam is a superb example of one who is reinventing his life with
purpose and passion after retirement.
Sam coaches couples through life transitions and fishes in the Gulf
of Mexico whenever he can.
Your**Legacy**Connection.com

When I first came to Florida at age 32, I was a self-confessed beach bum. Being semiretired at 32 or 82 introduces many interesting issues.

First, I needed to reinvent how I answered the question "So what do you do?" When I first arrived in Florida my answer was "I am a professional beach bum." Today my answer is quite different and has evolved into "I get paid to be creative each and every day." I mention that point now to bring your attention to the exciting opportunity you will have. Create an answer that includes what you are seeking most. Ironically, my answer almost always results in an interesting conversation that usually transforms itself into a friendship or business discussion. Your answer can also change day to day. If I am looking to advance my art career, I may answer, "I am an artist. If I am mostly seeking to sell my book I would answer, "I am an author".

Second, networking or meeting like-minded people can be difficult at first. I saw evidence of them all around me but I could not connect with them for some reason. The key to my not being able to connect with like-minded people was that my lifestyle was unconventional and untraditional. The people my age were all busy working and the people wandering the beach were all twice my age. Then someone in my path uttered the profound words I will not soon forget. A friend Meigs Glidewell said, "Invest in your community and your community will invest in you". That statement simply changed my focus, strategy, and profoundly my results. Today I am surrounded by an abundance of like-minded, powerful, creative and entrepreneurial friends. My business is booming and life is good! What did I do to connect with like-minded fascinating people? I volunteered at the Humane Society, joined Toastmasters, took up tap dancing, attended my weekly networking meetings, and wrote a book. Try any and everything.

If you wish to change your results, simply change your approach.

CreativityGuaranteed.com

Why is it that when some people retire they say "HURRAY" with fearless enthusiasm and energy"? Yet others say "Now what? Gosh, what am I supposed to do with the rest of my life?

When you retire, what will you say? How will you answer this question? *So what do you do*? Let us examine for a minute how you will answer that question. I have heard some interesting answers such as the following:

I am just retired

I have no idea

or Nothing

In my opinion, those answers are disempowering, self-defeating and uninspiring answers.

My personal answer to this question is "I am semi-retired and get paid to be creative everyday".

Create a powerful answer to the question.

So what do you do?

_____

Include your interests or hobbies. Tell others in that answer what you are looking for. Why tell someone you are a stay at home mom if you are most seeking to be a "mom-preneur" (definition - a

67

stay at home mom with a small business)?   A more powerful answer would be I am a stay at home mom with a small business making_____" You fill in the blank. The point here is to tell your audience something about what you are seeking. It matters not what it is, it simply matters that you communicate it clearly if you expect to get what you want.

Congratulations, You Got Fired!

Getting fired from a job is simply *forced change*. You may not be able to control getting fired or getting laid off, but you can control how you perceive it. When someone tells me they were fired, my response to them always is the same. I respond with genuine enthusiasm and say "*Congratulations!*" I tell them now you get to start anew and reinvent how you wish to make money. Maybe now you can create an environment that you actually like or love. Maybe now you can create coworkers with the same values and interests as yourself. Maybe now is the time to move to where you want to live.

Maybe now you can attract a career full of passion and purpose. What a simple concept. What a simple idea. Then why are the majority of people in our society not doing this? If that is you, please go to my website and read the *Free Advice* page for tips on what you can do today to start living your passion and purpose. I wish for you a balanced life, whatever your right balance is.

Balance

Most of the people I help through my coaching business come to me because they are out of balance. The tricky part about balance is that the correct or perfect balance formula is different everyday and is ever changing. There is no exact or science behind balance because we are forever changing and evolving. Even when you find your right balance circumstances and life can get in the way and throw you off. What I can offer about balance is to at least know what your ideals are surrounding these 7 key areas of your life. Create mission statements based on your goals and aspirations around these key areas;

Mind / Mental (Emotions)
Physical
Money and Finances
Friends, Family & Relationships
Career
Household
Spirituality

Another main strategy I use to find my perfect balance is to try everything once. Even if you end up not caring for that particular hobby or sport at least you tried it. "Better to have tried and failed, than not have tried at all". My "Sure, I'll try it" attitude has brought me to places I otherwise would not have ever seen or experienced. Here are a few I have tried: banging on drums in a drum circle, kayaking in the Gulf of Mexico, climbing the grand rapids in Jamaica, white water rafting in Costa Rica, dragon-boating, learning to bowl, snorkeling in the Bahamas, tap lessons and my most recent adventure-piano lessons. Whenever you are asked to try something new, just say Yes!

Find your passion and start making money from it.

Would you consider some of the following options?

Write a book?
Write an E Book?
Write for a newspaper?
Teach what you know to others?
Record a CD?
Sell your service or products on Ebay?
"Trade out" your services/products?
Become a consultant?

Sell your products at your home parties?

When some of my clients retired, the most challenging part was the emotional challenges that seem to come with the territory. I am not a mental-health expert, but I do know that when my clients apply some of those suggestions they begin to experience peace, balance and joy. Here are some suggestions for having a happy retirement experience.

Surround yourself with positive uplifting friends and family
Reinvent your *So what do you?* answer with a powerful one
Create a one-page retirement plan
(Email me for a free sample copy)
Create a health plan that addresses diet and exercise
Make time to relax
Develop a creative outlet
Spend some time alone every day
Give back to your community
Mentor someone in need of a positive influence
Find a way to leave a better world
Examine your beliefs and create new powerful ones
Have goals for three months, one year and five years

71

Share your expertise with others
Learn a new skill
Continuously be enrolled in a course
Travel the world
Read every day
Remove any negatives thoughts
Share your fortune with people you love
Find a passion, just one passion
Have a solid support system
Discover your purpose
Do something to improve your health each day
Have healthy empowering relationships
Strive for balance each day
Know what your perfect balance is
Learn to manage your expectations
Practice self-love and self-forgiveness
Leave a better world
Live your purpose every day
Find something to love every day
If all else fails, focus only on the good
Enjoy the *now*
Start a business doing what you love
And live where you wish to live

If you are not living where you truly desire,
develop a plan.

Find your passion and purpose and live it every day, and the world will become a better place.

This is a simple truth.

Painting by Artist Tracey Parnell
Acrylic on Canvass
Residing with Art Collector and Photographer Shelly Aldred

Reggie says
Do what you love, love what you do

*Creativity***Guaranteed**.com

Chapter 6

Is It Time to Start Your Own Small Business?

This chapter is dedicated to
Andy Rousseau
Andy exemplifies how to make millions of dollars while staying true
to ones purpose and passion.
Words to live by: "Live in the Moment" - Andy Rousseau

Start a Business and create multiple streams of income.

When money is a concern, you can take action with a few steps. First, examine your expenses and find current costs you can reduce or eliminate. *Trading* services is one of the quickest and most effective ways to do this. Ask 10 of your friends and you will find someone willing to trade his/her skill of haircutting for your craft of grass-cutting. Perhaps your doctor could use some of your original artwork for his/her office. Maybe your love of baking can be exchanged for house or dog-sitting.

I have several trade arrangements that include hair cutting, organizing, administration, computer hardware support and the list goes on and on. Trading services allows you to support your friends and family businesses while keeping your expenses down.

Another area that can be examined is your income. Regardless of your financial or employment status everyone can use an extra income stream. Developing multiple streams of income is a key to financial freedom. You simply travel and live where you wish while the multiple streams of income continue to flow into your bank account. It took me ten years of research to make this happen for myself but if I can do it anyone can. Having a website is as essential as having a business card. Websites now can be done for FREE. You need not be a software or computer genius. YAHOO is a simple and economical resource for building your own website.

Earn money from selling what you know or love to do. A woman I know, Nelly Camardo, has created a business from her passion. Nelly roams the beaches picking up rocks and seashells from the lovely shores of the Gulf of Mexico. She turns each find into a unique jewelry piece. Nelly then sells her jewelry at boutiques and craft shows. If you wish to see her beautiful one of a kind pieces

go to her website: www.bijeau.biz

Become a professional *whatever* and start a business. The bottom line and simple truth are that starting a business can cost as little as $60 to register it. As a traveling snowbird, it might be best to start the business in your country of origin. Any research, registration and payments can be done online. Starting a small business can be all about doing what you love to do: it does not always have to be focused on making millions. Any fear you have about starting or running a business is usually self-imposed false fear. I know that because I see clients' breakthrough this fear every day. Business owners I have coached invariably say to me "Why didn't you tell me it was this easy"? Of course, my response is, that is what I have been trying to tell you – you simply may not have been ready to hear such information at the time. Much of the stress associated with running a business is self inflicted.

The term "Professional" means is you have been paid to perform a service or provide a product. Retirement is a perfect time to share with others what you know and love. You can make a business of it by conducting seminars, selling workshops or even writing a book. Join a speakers bureau or get an agent that is motivated to get you professional speaking engagements-perhaps speaking about what you know and love.

Maybe you always wanted to open a business but have no idea what to do or offer. A friend of mine found the following to be her predicament. After struggling to find her passion, to no avail, she decided to sell products on eBay. How she came to that conclusion was by answering the question I often ask "*What do you love to do*"? Her answer was that she loves to have garage sales and also loves to play on the computer. She turned two of her loves into a viable business. The beauty of online businesses is that you can do them from virtually anywhere. I spend a lot of time with my computer sitting on the back of my boat, on a sandy beach or on an airplane. Selling on eBay takes a relatively short amount of training and offers a minimal learning curve. Selling other peoples stuff through eBay on consignment handles the potential problem of purchasing and housing expensive inventory.

Write a book

Writing a book is not as hard as you may think. I struggled when obtaining my high school diploma mainly due to the fact I despised math and English. Now if someone who does not excel in English is a published author (that would be me) then why not you? You need not be an English major or prolific writer you simply need a strong message and the proper tools and resources. Start by finding a message you want to share with others or simply share a success in your life and how you did it. Locate and hire the proper resources: an editor, publisher, ghostwriter, grammarian, printer and a marketer.

Ron Klein, www.The*Grandfather*of*Possibilities*.com
mentored me through the process of writing this book.

*Creativity*Guaranteed.com

Writers Block?

Ask for Help from the Experts!

Learn to write about what you know and write from your heart. Charles M. Bonasera www.CharlesmBonasera.com another friend and significantly important mentor and advisor provided me with a complimentary 30 minute coaching session that unleashed my inner author. Charles' offer is available to you as well, simply write or call him and mention my name. Charles' opened the flood gates by using some mental techniques and now I can't stop writing. I am currently writing a series of books.

The Coaches Coach 2010©
Yoga While You Work 2011©
101 Businesses a Teenager Can Start Today 2010©
and
Creativity into Cash 2011©

I explained the above because my limiting beliefs about writing were keeping me from becoming an author. Examine and change your beliefs about

*Creativity*Guaranteed.com

whatever you are most seeking. Examine your beliefs, tweak them, and then replace them with positive affirmations and you will attract all you desire. Guaranteed! Every person has at least one good book in them.

If you are not as independent as you might like to be and the thought of running a business makes you anxious, consider a creative solution. Maybe you don't like to work alone. Get an agent or representative. Obtaining someone such as an agent is much easier than one might think. I have several and have attained them all by simply approaching them one at a time. Each one of my agents has his/her area of expertise and they are not paid until I am paid. They are all independently seeking solutions and attracting clients for my businesses and investments. Agents are not only for movie stars and pop stars: they are for just about anything. Agents can be hired for writing books, marketing, artwork, and representing and acquiring you business for virtually any of your products and/or services. Having a team of agents working for you sure does lighten the load of running a business. When you have proper representation you can concentrate on what you do best and what you most enjoy.

Partnerships

Partnerships can work; however, in my experience the long term success rate of business partnerships is approximately 5 percent. If you are considering going into partnership, ask yourself, *Am I ready to marry this person?*

Invariably business partnerships result in an irreconcilable sad ending. While you may benefit from partnering up with someone who possesses admirable talents, I suggest you align or have some other type of an agreement, contract or arrangement instead. In that way, you can always either terminate or change your agreement as you evolve in your business without negatively affecting your core business. Partnerships are even more complicated and more damaging when with a close friend or marriage partner. Go it alone and get great supporters, mentors, and advisors. If your independence and freedom are at all important to you, consider going it alone.

Get good at spreading your word to individuals, but also to groups. Toastmasters International is one of the most inexpensive public speaking training programs offered. Join your local chapter and get good at delivering speeches. That skill will help you sell an idea or product to one person or a group of people. The networking benefits of joining and participating in such a group should not be overlooked either. Enhancing one's communication skills will improve any relationship you have and the ability to influence others. You can also find like-minded people through www.meetup.com.

Get a Mentor

Find some people living where you wish to live and ask them to mentor you through the process of relocating. Whatever you desire, find someone who has already done what you are seeking then simply ask them to show you the way. Of the thousands of people that have guided, coached or mentored me, not one person ever refused to help. You simply need to have the courage and forethought to ask the right questions.

It is also important to consider carefully who you will ask for help. Every single person learns and teaches differently. I watch, observe and take mental notes on who excels at what. Each person in my personal life acts as a teacher. I also reciprocate and offer lessons when and if they ask. Business aside for a moment, make this a reality with your friends and surrounding immediate world.

Real Life Proof

When I wrote this book I asked my mentor Charles Bonasera to rid me of writers block and he did in 30 minutes. It took me one year however to identify my issue, determine a trusted friend to ask and then to take action. When I stumbled through getting the book published I asked Ron Klein for help and he could not have been more helpful, effective and generous. I asked him only a few short months after meeting him in person. I spent two hours with Ron and was guided through the publishing world by an expert. I consider Ron an expert "at life" by the way not so much the publishing industry. While he knows a great deal about the publishing industry I think he would admit to not knowing all there is to know. One of the reasons I asked Ron to help me was I sincerely wanted to see how he mechanically got over around and under problems he encountered. And boy did I learn in those two short hours, how someone I consider to be a creative-genius, get what he wants in the end. I absorbed key success life lessons in the short time I spent with Ron Klein, TheGrandFatherofPossibilities.com.

*Creativity*Guaranteed.com

The last hurdle I faced when getting this book published was me, myself and I.   I was procrastinating...wait I will get back you later. lol (that means laugh-out-loud).

I found that I was stopping and stalling without a valid reason why. I recognized the issue like one would notice a hard to miss red stop sign. I then enlisted my trusted friend, mentor and communications expert Doug Ross. Doug spent a few hours with me walking through the publishing website. He was reminding me the key message I wish to offer you now. A success key is that each of us probably already knows what we want and how to get it. We are very good at knowing what it is we want however not always so good at the "getting" part.

The patience and generosity Doug gave me was exactly what I needed to hit the "PRINT" button.

Find someone who has done what you wish to accomplish and ask them how they did it.

*Creativity*Guaranteed.com

Thanks very much Doug!

www.Doug-Ross.com

Doug Ross, PhD

Collaborative Solutions Consulting

"I facilitate positive change!"

www.doug-ross.com

Books By Doug

http://www.dougross.webs.com/apps/webstore

*Creativity**Guaranteed**.com*

Goal Setting

When setting any goal in your life, it is most effective to consider this strategy. Use the S.M.A.R.T. Strategy. The SMART strategy is a way to set your goals so they include all these elements:

S   M   A   R   T
Specific, Measurable, Accountable, Realistic & Timely

Simply put, when you have a S.M.A.R.T. goal or strategy, you will turn your dreams into reality. It really can be that simple.

My S.M.A.R.T. goal was to live a healthy life in Florida for six winter months each year. I proclaimed that goal on the shores of Key West, Florida one year while gazing up at the stars with my feet firmly planted in the sand. I felt completely unaware of how that could happen. All I know is that once I proclaimed it and *surrendered* to not knowing how, it just magically happened. Is there something you long for, but are afraid to really dream about? Doctor Wayne Dyer calls it *manifesting your dreams*. Surrender to the fact you may not ever know *how* or *when* it will happen. Wayne calls it magic. Whatever you label it, I can tell you, it does work.

*Creativity*Guaranteed.com

When I recreated my life as a snowbird one of my desires was to not have to wear high heels every day to work. What would you do if money was not your number one priority?

Tracey taking a break while shooting a wedding on the beach.
Proof that you can create a *no heels required* career.
CreativityGuaranteed.com/photography

If you are a business person you are more likely to identify more with a word such as strategy when talking about obtaining what you want. Let's look for a moment at strategizing.

Strategizing, plotting, planning, or scheming can all be about looking at something from an objective point of view. It is when we look at a desire or calling more objectively. It can be profoundly more helpful to use other people to

*Creativity*Guaranteed.com

help you this area. Collect a group of trusted people and ask them to help you brainstorm your goals. Create a strategy around your goals and desires.

I like to think of strategizing as being similar to the game of chess. The moves are strategies and the actual chess pieces are goals. You need all the chess pieces present and lined up first. Then is it not the moves (strategies) that win or lose the game? Of course, it is.

S=Systematic
T=Tenacity
R=Research
A=Attitude
T=Timely
E=Expectations
G=Goals
Y=Your Mission Statement

Sailors strategy was to find perfect parents.
Rich and Rita are as close as you get.

*Creativity***Guaranteed**.com

My strategy around becoming a snowbird was the following:

Travel to Florida during the winters to research housing and employment options. Take up to 3-6 months off each year in Florida to write a series of books. Create multiple streams of income in Canada that will support the lifestyle I desire. Develop daily disciplines that will result in a healthy snowbird lifestyle.

Start a Small Business

Announce it and shout it out

If you wish to start a business, consider these inexpensive options to spread the word:

- Radio (find a station to interview you).
- Newspaper (invite the editor to interview you).
- Television – Send a press release and personal invitation to the on air anchors / producers and media representatives – Target the anchors that specialize in the same topics that you are featuring or highlighting.
- Magazines accept contributing writings or announcements.

90

- Write to the features editor, writers and columnists of your local newspaper and send them a personal invitation to share your story
- When all else fails, use the internet, and use Google, to search for whatever you are seeking

Get a Coach

I was an incompetent boss myself before I was properly trained. Most people are very ill suited to becoming an effective leader. Human emotions and sabotage become factors when trying to survive in the workplace. Most working conditions are rated average to below average. That leaves the responsibility to the individual. We can create our ideal working environment with some creative thinking and action. When I hired my first coach, the coaching industry was new and my company did not endorse and pay for her services. I creatively found several ways to get the coaches I desired.

When you ask for help it lightens the load tremendously. The trick to finding your right coach is to seek someone you admire and ask for help. No one has ever refused to help me.

Pierre Robitaille, is one of my mentors who inspired and equipped me with everything I needed to leave the corporate world comfortably.
I am forever grateful to him because as I am now living what I only once dreamt about.
Photographer unknown

Whether you are working in a corporation or small business you should consider becoming very deliberate with *your own* personal career path. As an employee you are paid to serve, attain and fulfill the corporate mission. The most content and successful people I know are ones who have planned their own career paths in consultation with a mentor.

You can make strategic moves to climb the corporate ladder but you should have someone other than your boss guiding you along the way. Your direct boss will have his or her own motivations behind promoting or steering you. You can have much difficulty in navigating your career alone. Find a coach, mentor or leader outside your immediate working environment to help navigate effectively through the corporate waters.

One might consider having experts to rely on in these following areas;

Accounting/Bookkeeping
Advertising
Affiliate Marketing
Business
Chiropractic
Client Acquisition & Retention
Computer Hardware
Education
Entrepreneurship
Finances
Internet – Affiliate Marketing
Internet
Computer - Software
Legal Matters
Marketing
Non-Traditional Medicine
Traditional Medicine
Nutrition
Personal Trainer
Psychotherapy
Security
Spirituality

When you have the experts in your corner, nothing can keep you to achieving any goal.

My clients, with whom I work with, that, are the most content and joyful are the ones who have created a career around their passions in life, and not the other way around.

Not being very happy at work is common today and most people simply just live with it? As the 5 o'clock bell rings, off they run, convinced there is nothing they can do about their misery other than temporarily escape. For the most part I have had incredible leaders for me to follow, but of course have had my share of bosses that were emotionally and verbally abusive. The truth as I see now is that those individuals were simply not happy about life in general. Some would add insult to injury by stealing my ideas and inventions and presenting them as their own. I used that fact to ignite in me the need and desire to get out of that job or corporation even faster than originally anticipated. The statement I repeated silently was "*I will be my last boss*". To this day, I still am my own boss. I now refuse to work for any one individual and remain to be my own boss. If you can relate to my former situation or you are currently stuck there, I suggest create an exit strategy fast. Having an exit strategy is not only empowering, it is wonderfully liberating.

Donald Trump inspired me to redirect my focus of "the bad boss syndrome" into creating a life of passion and purpose. Donald says "The best revenge is living well", I choose to take his advice.

Restlessness is discontent and discontent is the first necessity of progress. Show me a thoroughly satisfied man and I will show you a failure.
Thomas A. Edison

If your motivation to relocate is because of a bad boss be sure that when you move into a new position, you do not attract another ill-suited person to report to. This can be easily discovered through the interview process. Starting your own company is an alternative to having to deal with office politics and bad bosses. Consider getting a myriad of free training programs offered through the government. You may also inquire at the company of which you are currently employed for training courses offered. To find them simply go online. Google is a wonderful resource.

If you do start a small business, make sure the product is something you love- get paid to perform your hobby. Once you work out the initial kinks of a small business, you will be able to play every day and be paid to do so. When registering a business you need to adhere to the local regulations. It is against the law to work in any country that is not your country of origin without the proper work visas or permits.

I turned my hobby of yoga into a revenue stream simply by offering to teach others.
Above, Tracey teaches a stretch class to students on a floating dock in Toronto, Canada.
Photography by Robert Foster

My three businesses have afforded me the opportunity to be paid to be creative, have fun and be my own boss. Are you suited to be a small business owner? To take a free test check www.CreativityGuaranateed.com

Chapter 7

The Nay Sayers

Dedicated to Rick Stewart
Rick has taught me many life lessons that are largely responsible for my lifestyle today. Rick unselfishly shares his wisdom and has empowered me with knowledge that made me truly fearless. Rick taught me how to be compassionate.
Words to live by:
"When others choose to ignore you, simply enjoy the peace" and "Consider the source" – Rick Stewart

Making the choice to spend your winters in a warmer climate is not the norm, especially for those significantly under the normal retirement age. People, at first, and even to this day, question my lifestyle choice. Being a snowbird living - where I choose and when I choose - is the most empowering choice I have made in my lifetime. I live everyday in amazement that I get to live a never-ending summer. I live in Florida six winter months (less one day), and then return to my home in Canada for the summer. I truly get the best that both worlds have to offer. When it is time to return to my Canadian home in the spring, the timing could not be more perfect. The birds are singing the flowers are blooming and, best of all, my friends and family are all in high spirits and happy as can be to see my return. Where is *your* paradise?

Consider the Source

There are people who live permanently in what I call EmptyVille. Those are the types of people who will tell you all the reasons you should *not* do something or point out what is *wrong*. They are experts at pointing out the negative but can still offer you value—*if you learn to use and manage it.* That is a skill that, once developed, can be applied to all negative feedback. You can simply do one of two things here. One positive thing you can do is flip the negative reason into a positive one. For example, you will have to quit your job. Try this more positive statement, "you *get* to quit your crummy job and reinvent who you are by seeking out your purpose and passion".

The second positive action you can take concerning negative feedback is that you can ensure you have a solution in place if the *what if* were to occur such as-what if the car breaks down, what if the house deal falls through, what if a tornado crosses your path? Those are situations for which you may simply prepare for. That plan can be made while still maintaining a positive mindset. Do your research prior to your departure and have an escape or backup plan for any such event. Knowing the proper authorities

98

to contact in the event of an emergency can offer much reassurance and comfort.

When you *consider the source* it is helpful to be aware that when your naysayers hear words such as freedom, snowbird, and living abroad, it may trigger their own fear and limitations. To you, those words likely represent excitement, fun and intrigue. To them those words may represent feelings such as abandonment, loss or personal failure. Provoking the acknowledgement of true feelings is a powerful and liberating skill.

I have to say that I have had many naysayers on my journey, in particular, when recreating my life as a snowbird. Many people had a hard time understanding my lifestyle choices. I wish to simply say now *Thank you*. Each negative comment or judgmental gaze has only empowered me to move forward that much sooner. I caution you to expect that not everyone will *get your plan*. If you use the negativity as ammunition, fuel to feed your positive enthusiasm, there will be no stopping you. That is an effective life strategy when attempting to reach any goal.

The other powerful realization I came to when managing naysayers is that often your audience is simply rejecting the idea and not you personally. One year, while navigating Homeland Security at the Ambassador Bridge crossing in the United States, an immigration inspector temporarily detained me. The officer actually telephoned my partner to confirm my Canadian status and my somewhat hard-to-believe-story. It seemed incomprehensible to the officer that we could be a *couple* and yet spend so many months apart. When she asked the question of my partner over the phone, he replied "Quite frankly, Inspector, we find that the separation has greatly contributed to the longevity of our relationship." He is quite the comedian. After spending several hours confirming other facts about my unconventional lifestyle, the inspector reluctantly, but lawfully, granted me entrance to the United States. She did nothing to make me feel welcome as I crossed the border. Another lesson I learned and practice is the following. *Others can make you feel something only if you allow it.*

Naysayers simply point out the negatives due to their own personal limitations and fears. The moment you recognize and acknowledge that fact the better off you will be. I know I cannot control others thoughts or actions but I can control what I allow to come into my world and mind. When presented with negativity, I choose to refocus my energy inward. I simply ask myself "What can I do to show this person how to live a life of purpose and passion?" The answer usually is, live your own life of purpose and passion and that may lead others simply by example. The best example to offer is living-well.

Are you a naysayer? We all can be at times. Have you heard the famous saying "You are your own worst enemy"? Are you reading this thinking, *Yes this is all fine and good for others, but not for me?* From time to time we can all be naysayers or be in a negative and doubtful place. I would like to suggest that you turn your doubt into action by developing an exit strategy for yourself.

Make your plan for one year or 10 years time from now. The pressure might ease when you do that. You can turn your own negative thoughts of *No* into How will I do this when the time is right? If you start by simply exclaiming *I am retiring and moving to California in 5 years*, the energy and space takes on a new life.

Timing is Important

Some of my friends and clients who wish to live in a warm climate simply cannot do it now. They have the awareness and desire to create the lifestyle of a snowbird but it is simply not the right time for them. I recommend they focus on what they can do now, for when the timing *is right*.

Redirecting your energy into an action plan is incredibly uplifting and freeing. One of the clients I have says "I am living the life of a snowbird in seven years, eight months, five days (and depending on how bad the rat race is that particular day, he may also include how many *hours* as well).

Another powerful idea I now carry with me, thanks to THE BIG IDEA with Donny Deutsch on CNBC, is the following:

The word
NO
simply means **Not** Yet!

That is a helpful belief to adopt whether you are trying to convince someone of an idea or sell a product.

Chapter 8

Legalities

Behind every Law is a reason.
Is the reason right or wrong?
Who is to say?
Ignorance is not accepted, knowing and following the laws makes
for a simpler life.
Tracey Parnell
www.CreativityGuaranteed.com

Border Crossing

The immigration laws can easily be honored and followed while living where you wish to live. Each country and laws are different, of course, and you need to find out the laws and adhere to them. Each time I crossed the border to my U.S. home, I simply told them I was going to visit family for three to six months. I sometimes had less than a positive experience at the border. Border officials once detained me for questioning for three hours until finally they realized I was simply doing something unconventional and not illegal. The border experiences actually gave me some ammunition to write this book. Thanks, guys!

Canadian federal and provincial laws permit one to leave the country for six months less one day, in order to retain residency and OHIP (Ontario

Health Insurance Plan) benefits. Any of the information I offer should be verified with the proper authorities. Legislation is time sensitive, new laws, and amendments seem to be proclaimed almost daily.

Finances

If you are struggling in any way with your finances I suggest one simple, powerful thing to try. I believe the very first thing you should observe and consider is changing *your outlook or beliefs* about money. Clearly, if you had effective beliefs about money, you would be now living where you wish to live year-round. Maybe you are living exactly where you wish currently - If so, congratulations. Please, however, allow me to make a blanket assumption since you are reading this book, you are seeking change. Beliefs about money do one of two things, they attract money or they do not. Please answer the following question.

I believe it will require more money than I am currently spending to live in two homes or locations. YES or NO

One of my objectives is to prove the answer to that question is NO.

Beliefs can be uncovered by the thoughts going through our heads. What are your thoughts and beliefs about money?   Are they something like any of the following beliefs?

I attract all the money I desire

People wish to give me money unconditionally

There is an infinite amount of money on this planet for me and everyone

Money is easy to attain

I am able to help others as I have unlimited money

Money is ever flowing

I spend money easily

If you are not having those empowering thoughts, consider adopting them at least for a week and see what happens.   If you are still struggling simply email me and I will send you a free belief buster exercise by mail. Tracey@CreativityGuaranteed.com

This exercise is an example of creating affirmations. If you repeat them on a continual basis, you will attain what you have decided to focus on. Focus on *lack* and you will be left wanting. Focus on *abundance* and *abundance* will be your result. You decide!

Money - Fast Track Tips

Monitor your expenses (eliminate or reduce)
Develop multiple streams of income
(This book is one example of my own multiple streams of income)
Create affirmations and install new beliefs in your thinking
Find or create a borderless job or way to make money
Trade out services and products with others

Money Tips

When you live in paradise year-round your need for a vacation simply vanishes. The money you would normally spend on a two week vacation will now get you two months when you live abroad. The key fact to know about travel and living part time is that when you are on vacation, your budget can be up to five times what it would cost if you were a local.

106

My trip to the islands when I worked in the corporate rat race was about $2000 for a 10-day trip. When I relocated, that same $2000 covered me for two months. Do the math and see how long your dollar can stretch. The prices are much different for travelers than they are for the locals. You want to be considered a local. This secret is a key to understanding how you can get local prices instead of being treated as a tourist.

This became clear to me when I spent months in Costa Rica. I was sent to the local farmers market to buy our family's weekly fruits and vegetables. You see I am dark skinned and the local farmers and vendors assumed I was Spanish speaking local. I was therefore given rock bottom prices. When I took along anyone who appeared as if s/he was a tourist, the prices suddenly doubled. This is not an illegal act, only a fun quirk one may experience in different cultures.

Financial Freedom

Yeah! Right! Financial freedom is possible and can be achieved, but the sooner you start the better. I had a boss once tell me that and, thankfully, I seriously considered his advice and took action. The action I took at a young 22 years of age has contributed largely to the lifestyle I live today.

Thanks in part to Robert Kiyosaki and his book *Rich Dad Poor Dad* I learned the success laws of financial freedom.

1. Diversify your investments.
2. Take small steps each day for your long-term financial plan.
3. Readdress your financial situation every three months.
4. Cut your losses on losing investments sooner, rather than later.

Debt
Living south has forced me to investigate my finances. Either you increase your income or reduce your expenses. I investigated for ten years how to make money online. There are literally thousands of ways to do just this.

Insurance
Many insurance companies see snowbirds as desirable clients and often offer favorable pricing. Please know that the snowbird insurance industry is complex and highly specialized. This means you should not decide on a provider based on

108

price alone. Always consider all the services that you will require.

Be sure you have all your insurance needs covered travel, health, pet, home, auto and life.

I have heard that some ill-intended insurance companies have deliberately not communicated all the parameters of the policies they offer to snowbirds. Of course, if that is true I assume that that would be done for greed purposes only. One thing I think we can all agree on is *get it in writing:* insist on having a clearly written copy of the policy outline.

Financial planning should include the following six items:

1. tax planning,
2. banking,
3. currency fluctuations,
4. retirement income,
5. financial planning, and
6. investment & brokerage services.

Your best bet is to tell all your advisors what you are planning to do. I simply went to my bank and explained how long I would be gone and they offered me easy solutions. I was able to address all my above-mentioned issues in two simple meetings.

Even though snowbirds are healthier than ever (perhaps because of being a snowbird), wellness issues rank high in the list of interests for snowbirds. Be sure you consider the wellness issues so that your extended trip is free from illness and full of wellness and fun. See your doctor to be sure you have all your prescriptions for your extended vacation. (Be certain you explain your extended plans because drug interactions have been known to occur)

Place a note in your file with your doctor that you will be on extended vacation and may be calling in the event of an emergency. Check for the need for any vaccines and such.

Wellness generally improves because of the simple fact you are living were you wish to live. Take note this might be the time to kick the habit and finally quit a smoking habit, or perhaps reach your ideal weight goal.

When we change our surroundings, especially for the better, this sets the perfect stage for positive change. Breaking or creating a habit can be a great deal easier to implement when you are in unfamiliar but empowering surroundings.

They say it takes 21 consecutive days to form or break a habit.

Safety can be of particular importance when traveling to unknown territories. Take precautions to be personally safe and take measures to safeguard your personal belongings and property. Consider carefully what to take with you. Where will you store your passport and cash? I particularly like the freezer for a hiding spot. Well, until now, that is, now that I have revealed this tip publicly. High end electronics can be camouflaged in non identifying travel cases and luggage. Take a full circle walk around your vehicle before leaving it and make sure it is secure and unappealing to a thief.

When considering safety in general, get creative, use common sense, and most of all tell no one whatever what your strategy is. A movie I watched recently had a burglar say "snowbirds are an easy target", when referring to performing home invasions. I am not a fan of pointing out anything negative but let's face it, we have to consider all the angles if we wish to be safe at all times.

Zoee is a Snowbird wannabee
Bringing your pet?
Be sure you have all their papers and medical history

Canadian SnowBirds in training
Julie and David Gallagher
BirthExperience.com
www.best biz.ca

*Creativity***Guaranteed**.com

Chapter 9

Invest in Your Community

I gratefully dedicate this chapter to a long time friend, confidant and business mentor George Habib. George is a man who has abundant creativity, generosity and brilliance. George is a constant reminder to me that one can still succeed and prosper while giving back and creating a better community.
Words to live by:
"Nurture your relationships, foster new ones, and give back to your community." - George Habib

Invest in your community, and your community will invest in you. When I first became a snowbird, I had a challenging time meeting like-minded people. I was going against the grain so to speak. The people of my age and with my interests were all working. As I roamed the beaches, I ran into other snowbirds, but clearly not people my own age. I met some interesting people along the way, no doubt, but still had a yearning to be with people in my age range that shared similar interests. Are you surrounded with empowering and inspiring friends and colleagues? Consider the art of meeting people and forging new relationships just that - an art. An art you can learn to get good at.

Whenever I am stuck on an issue or problem, I ask 10 people for their opinion. Usually one, if not more has the answer I am seeking. The best therapist or counselor is the one that resides in oneself.

Fake It, until You Create It.

If you do not have what you want (whether a job, snowbird status, or whatever), try what I call *Fake it until you create it*. At the next social function you attend, when asked, you can answer with what it is you are seeking now. *My name is Tracey and I am a snowbird.* Some may say doing that before *it* has happened could be construed as lying. My belief is *I can see into my future and that timeframe matters not*. This is especially valid when we are talking about manifesting our dreams.

When you talk about *it* like it already exists, something magical happens. It is as effective as positive visualization. I have used that technique when creating myself into a photographer, artist, motivational speaker, coach, producer, director, author and soon to be self made millionaire.

Copycat

Before becoming a snowbird, I very much disliked when I was forcefully guided onto a plane to fly home to Canada during the winter months. Knowing the snow was waiting patiently would make me feel trapped and compromised. Instead of residing with that fact I would daydream of a life I knew could and would be better. I used examples such as Joe Walsh from the Eagles, Jimmy Buffet, Cheryl Crow and James Taylor to inspire me. Each of them is an example of living a life of passion and purpose. Find those who are already doing what you want and emulate them. Investigate to find how they did each and every task to end up living a life of passion and purpose. Break it down to simple daily tasks you can do to achieve the life you want. Commit yourself to complete ONE simple task each day. If you miss one day do two the next to make up for it and dwell only on the positive. Remain focused on the outcome of your goal and sure go ahead and obsess about it until it becomes a reality.

Invest in your community and your community will invest in you. These words have given me many positive results. When you first relocate, like-minded friends may be hard to find at first. I have met several friends and business associates through my volunteerism at the Humane Society or various other non-profit groups.

Are you personable? Develop your people skills. More importantly are you memorable? Did you know it takes between three and seven interactions before the average person will remember you, your name or what you do?

Seven Steps *to be remembered*

1. 3 - 5 minutes is the maximum time that most people can listen intently and fully before their attention wanders (use one method of communication for a maximum three minutes – then change your communication style) or move on to meeting another person.

2. Use a minimum of two communication styles when meeting someone (visual, storytelling, and/or verbal/instructional).

3. Engage your listener – ask questions.

4. Prove that you are listening (restate what they have said).

5. Offer ideas and free resources to show you are willing to help and are paying attention to them.

6. Use the mirroring technique – essentially this means to mimic the other person's body language, tone and rhythm.
Like attracts Like

7. Be funny, have a joke or funny story in your pocket.

Networking

Disarm yourself–tell a personal story - share something comical about yourself. When meeting someone new it is advantageous to show them that you are by no means perfect or of higher status or importance. When we break down a wall by using that technique, communication becomes easy and enjoyable. Try this in your next meeting or interview.

"Invest in Your Community and Your Community Will Invest in You"

Never were truer words spoken than the heading above. While in Florida, I decided to volunteer at the Humane Society since I have a passion for dogs. Then I joined a bowling team and later Toastmasters. Toastmasters became a wise career choice. Six short years later, I became a professional motivational speaker. At the time, I joined Toastmasters only to meet like-minded people. Not only did I meet like-minded people, but it also advanced my professional career by leaps and bounds. Toastmasters International is a club that can advance any career you may have. Once a member, you are entitled to go to any chapter meeting worldwide.

If you are searching for a life mate, a friend or just people to meet, consider volunteering at a non-profit organization. You may need to volunteer for a few groups before you find the right fit. Go online or to your local church to discover the myriad of non-profit organizations.

Take a class at a local technical institution or school. After years of apprenticing with photographers, then investing in the proper equipment, I decided to take photography classes. I not only met some new friends at the world-renowned Ringling School of Art & Design, I became a professional photographer. Photography has become another one of my passions. I now get paid to take photographs. What do you love to do?

Blue Jay at work was my very first attempt as a professional photographer.
Photograph by Tracey Parnell (Ontario, Canada), student of Elena De La Ville, www.edelaville.com

Photography is another hobby I turned into a revenue stream. Discover what you love to do, and then find a way to get paid too do it.

Professional means you get paid to perform a service. What kind of professional can you become? Use your snowbird time off to research, rephrase and reinvent who you are. Develop or sharpen your skill set.

"I get to shoot what I love to look at"
Tracey Parnell, Photographer

119

I personally enjoy taking photographs of all my dogs when they are playing.
Photograph by Tracey Parnell (Mac's Row, Ontario, Canada)

Tuscany takes some time to herself.
Photograph by Tracey Parnell (Mac's Row, Ontario, Canada)

*Creativity*Guaranteed.com

Create a business card. Even if you are retired, make yourself a business card if you expect to forge any relationships. You can go online to www.VistaPrint.com and get 250 business cards free. You simply pay approximately $5 for shipping. If you get stuck designing your business card, simply send me an email. All my clients get free business cards! You can have your cards created and designed by one of my graphics staff members. Simply send me an email with the content you wish to see on your business card and we will design it and ship it directly to you.*

*All you need to pay is for the shipping. (Average cost is $5)

Why do I offer that? Part of my passion and purpose is to empower others. Every day I see people getting what they want from simply having and presenting a business card. That is why I make this offer. I wish to see you get what you desire. It is really that simple.

Tracey@CreativityGuaranteed.com
*while supplies last

When I go to any party or event, I use the *power of three*. Meet at least three people and

CreativityGuaranteed.com

exchange business cards. Also offer my business card only when asked. My preference is to make tangible and meaningful connections. I am motivated for *quality* connections not *quantity*.

Are parties not your thing? Online websites for meeting others are plentiful. Perform a Google search to find a club of interest. Churches and local libraries are also a great place for meeting others. The library has several government-funded courses you can take. Most, if not all, computer courses or *listen to the author* are free. Go, listen, and talk to the people around you. Meetup.com is a great free website.

Y.E.S. (Young Entrepreneurs of Sarasota) www.YES941.com is a group I joined that is a *not-for-profit* support group for entrepreneurs. That group has been a tremendous source of support, ideas, and encouragement for me and about 1000 other members. Find groups that will help you realize your dreams and goals. Whether you have an invention you wish to take to market or simply like to knit or sew recreationally, finding like-minded people will enhance your life. By simply participating, listening and taking action of the advice offered at Y.E.S., I literally doubled my business in size.

Find Like-Minded People, they come in all shapes, ages and sizes.

Here is an example of a 9 year old entrepreneur.
She makes "little people" out of clay.
Here she is selling one of her creations at a tradeshow in Florida.
Photography by Tracey Parnell. 9 year old Entrepreneur–unknown

Join a Group of Like Minded People

The co-founder of Y.E.S. John Greer is a business owner and entrepreneur at heart. John tirelessly leads our Y.E.S. group meetings as a contribution to our community. John is known as our Y.E.S. fearless leader and continues to create a better community by generously giving his expertise and time. John's *can-do* attitude reminds us all to not only ask the right questions

123

but as John would say, "At YES the answer is always YES". Regardless of your income status or geographic location; giving back simply creates a better world. What are you doing or can you do to leave a better world?

John Greer Auto Sales
www.jgas.us and co-founder of YES941.com
www.YES941.com
Photographer Unknown

Acting is a passion, Jonathan Greer Jr

Chapter 10

The How to Logistics

This chapter is dedicated to Dan and Willie Banting.
Dan and Willie are living proof that perseverance and hard work
pays off in the end.
They are both happily retired, living as snowbirds after successful
careers.
Both Dan and Willie have encouraged and inspired me to live my
life with passion and purpose.

Are you snowbird material? Consider the following questions.

1. I am comfortable with change. YES/NO
2. New places, people, and scenery excite me. YES/NO
3. The thought of moving some of my belongings is somewhat intriguing. YES/NO
4. I have one or more hobbies I can do virtually anywhere. YES/NO
5. My friends and family are willing to travel to see me. YES/NO
6. I am interested in expanding or starting a new business. YES/NO
7. I am good at creating and seeking solutions. YES/NO
8. My family and friends support me. YES/NO

*Creativity*Guaranteed.com

9. The thought of finding my passion and purpose excites me? YES/NO
10. My business can survive without *me* physically in it. YES/NO

If you answer yes to three or more of the questions above, you just might be a likely snowbird candidate.

Transportation Alternatives

My transmission blew up thank you very much! Really, this happened to me a one past winter five days before I was to head south. My car was fully packed for the winter trip with all my belongings safely stowed when that occurred. My brother Andy (my trustful and honest mechanic as well) informed me of that fact. I looked at this occurrence as a business problem. I asked, "Is it time to let go of my car or is it worth putting good money into an already aging car?" I decided to let it go, I then scrapped the car. I turned to my reliable friend the internet and searched *Toronto, Florida, drive, car* and about one million hits came up. I called the first three and within two days, I lined up a car to drive to Florida. My departure date was bumped by only two simple weeks.

My problem became my opportunity! The quality of the question on which I focused was, *how can this be possible*? I did not consider anything else. I knew I was going to my Florida home, one way or another. It is the *certainty* you feel that propels you into action. Therefore, with a *trains, planes and automobile* attitude, I got what I knew was certain.

Not only did I solve the problem of transporting myself to Florida, I eliminated a cost. There are many companies that need drivers to drive cars one way and they simply cover the cost of the gas and travel expenses.

www.TorontoDriveaway.com is a company that
has drivers transport cars
to Florida, Arizona and Toronto.

With gas prices as they are virtually everyone is seeking transportation alternatives. I know CEOs of corporations that make over one million dollars annually, but they use public transportation and refuse to own a car. Why you might ask? The rich are rich for a reason. They tend to research and then do what makes most economic sense. They do this regardless of public opinion or judgment.

Whether you wish to create an alternative method of transportation to save the environment or you wish to save money, thinking outside the box for your transportation needs is a perspective worth considering.

Consider these other transportation alternatives such as the following:

Rent a car
(Hertz has a $5 a one-way deal)
Buy a bike at the beginning of your stay and sell it or store it when you leave town
Find someone already traveling to your destination and offer to carpool
Transport Companies are often seeking "casual labor drivers"
Share a car (three days a week you use the car and your spouse or partner has it for the rest of the week)
Other people's automobiles
Motorcycle
Fly one way
Get hired to be an airline courier
(to deliver important documents via air)
Train

The most powerful message I wish to impress upon you is that you begin to think creatively.

Think *outside the box* as to how you can get whatever you are seeking. Focus only on the positive. Keep changing the quality of your questions until you get what you want. Dismiss any negativity. If you can master this skill, you will create an entire life you desire and love. Kurt Wright taught me this valuable lesson through his book. *Breaking the Rules*, by Kurt Wright is a truly life changing book that transformed the way I approach virtually every business issue.

Rather than listing a host of websites that may be outdated and no longer active by the time you come to do your research and perhaps read this book, please just consider the following ideas. Use the internet and make Google your friend. Simply type in the search field, in three or fewer words, what it is you are most seeking. If you do not have a computer or computer skills, take a trip to your local library and ask for help. Librarians can be among the most pleasant and friendly new friends you can make.

Ask ten people your question or share your elevator speech. Ask, *how can I make this happen*? Now simply take action. I hope to see you on the beach one day soon.

This book includes a free 15-minute telephone consultation with myself or a representing agent, and is valid up to one year from the time of purchase, Long-distance charges may apply.

I sincerely hope that you create a life of passion and purpose. Decide today to live in paradise year-round. There is plenty of space for us all.

The sun, she awaits.

Tracey Parnell
CreativityGuaranteed.com
The 40 Year Old Snowbird
SnowBirdsofSarasota.ning.com
Photography by Daniel Dutka, Toronto Photographer

130

"How To" Action Plan

Determine your desired location.

Negotiate Rent or Lease for housing.

Communications requirements (cellular, landline, long distance, internet).

Contact Travel and Tourism for E-Newsletters or mailings.

Check weather channel for patterns and trends.

Transportation - prepare for alternative or safety.

Contact Police Department for statistics on crime and other local issues.

Determine dates of travel.

Doctor Appointment (medications for your extended absence).

Dentist Appointment.

Have all personal Identification updated (mainly passport).

Photocopy your personal ID twice (keep back up in safe place).

Budget how much money you will require and be aware of currency fluctuations.

Determine how you will access or obtain money while abroad.

Photograph your entire home and valuable belongings.

Have your destination's full address with you when cross the border.

Hire a company for mail, snow removal and home inspection.

Know your spending limit when returning to Country of Origin (border laws).

Contact to inform of your extended vacation your;
- ✓ Banker
- ✓ Accountant
- ✓ Financial advisor
- ✓ Insurance Providers (automobile, life, boat, RV and health)
- ✓ Doctor / Dentist
- ✓ Postal Worker
- ✓ Cellular communications provider
- ✓ Home phone and cable

Packing List

Automobile Records / Files
Beach Accessories
Book
Camera
Cellular or communications devises
Clothing
Entertainment Equipment (iPod, videos)
Food
Hobby supplies (fishing rod, paint…)
Insurance Records / Files
Jewelry watch (keep in mind security)
Keys
Laptop / Computer / Printer
Magazines
Medical Records / Files
Medications
Music
Passport & Identification
Reading Material
Sporting Equipment
Toiletries

References and Resources

Thanks to my Advisory Board, I have obtained over 5000 hours of training and development. The following courses, books, and teachers can be found online.

7 Keys to Happiness, Tee and Trish Ross
A Whole New Mind, Daniel Pink
All I really need to know I learned in Kindergarden, Robert Fulghum
Amy Sky, International Singer & Entertainer
And What Do You Do? Loretta Kaufman and Mary Quigley
APTinternational.org
Art of Negotiating, University of Toronto
Assessment.com
Association for Psychological Type
Attracting Perfect Customers, Stacey Hall & Jan Brogniez
Audience Analysis, Career Systems
Be Who You Want to Be, Doug Ross, PhD
Beach Money, Jordan Adler
Behavioral Interviewing, Isabell Briggs
Ben Johnson
Bob Izumi
Bob Panasik
Brain Works
Breaking The Rules, Kurt Wright
BreakOutoftheBox.com

Creativity a New Psychology, George Swede
Darryl Godreau
Darryl Sittler
Dave Devall
David Cassidy
David Dunbar
David Jaffer
Dealing with Difficult People, Frontline Leadership
Dealing with Emotional Behavior, Frontline Leadership
Delegation and Team Management, University of Toronto
Diane Lane
Discover Your Strengths, MarcusBuckingham.com
Dixie Chicks, Juno Award Show
Don Cherry
Don Martin
Doug Flutie
Dr. Wayne Dyer
Drake Predictive Performance Profile, Inc.
E Myth Mastery, Michael E. Gerber
Elfie Schlegel
Elvis Stojko
Enneagram Institute.com
Fashion Show Production, Humber College of Applied Arts & Technology
Full Color Living/Work, Jennifer Joy Walker
Get Out of Your Own Way, Mark Goulston, M.D.
GetMotivated.com

Giving and Getting Feedback, Beverly Berstein and Beverly Kaye
Gordon James
Grief to Grace, Angela Scaefers
Guide for Managing Your Career, Ken Lawson
Hal Johnson
Hay House, Inc.
His Holiness, The Dahli Lama
How to Survive in Difficult Times, David Owen Ritz
Howie Mandel
Hugh Wakeham
Ian Miller
IMG
Interview Skills Coach
Jack Masterson, M.D.
Jeff Adams
Jim Dygert, CEO Space
Jim McKenney
Jim Ralph
Jim Tatti
Joanne McLeod
JobHuntersBible.com
Joe Bowen
Joe Carter
Jonathan Welsh
Jon Burnside
Josee Chouinard
Julianne Gillies, Miss Toronto
Junior Achievement International

Karen Stemmle
Kay Worthington
Ken Clark
Ken Shaw
Kurt Browning
Lance Brown
Larry Fedoruk
Laura Hollister
Laurie Graham
Law of Attraction, Esther and Jerry Hicks
Life Balance for a Working Woman, Career Track
Life Is a Series of Presentations, Tony Jeary
Lisa Alexander
Managing Multiple Priorities, Pryor Resources Inc.
Marc Chambers
MarcusBuckingham.com
Marilyn Dennis
Mark McKoy
Marketing & Advertising Certification, Humber College
of Applied Arts & Technology
Marnie McBean
Meeting Planning & Conference Planning
Certification, George Brown of Applied Arts
Melissa Ann DeMarco
Michael Burgess
Michael Collymore
Michael Smith
Michelle Wright Band
Michelle Wright, Canadian Country Music Awards

Mike Mandel

Monika Deol

Motivational Appraisal of Personal Potential

Myers-Briggs Type Indicator

Negrita Jayde

Nic Sansalone

One Minute Sales Person, Spencer Johnson, M.D.

Oprah Winfrey

Pat Foram

Patty Goble

Patty Loveless

Paul Coffey

Paul Henderson

Paul Molodar

Peel Regional Police

Personality Type Profiling, Isabel Briggs

Pierre Vercheval

Professional Resource Exchange, Inc.,

Psychological Assessment Resources, Inc.

Resolving Team Conflicts

Revitalizing Retirement, Nancy K. Schlossberg EdD

Rex Smith

Rickie Henderson

RileyGuide.com

Ringling School of Art, Photography

Rob Crowder

Rob Rouse

Robert Redford

Roberta Bondar

Roberto Alomar
Robin Ward
Rock Thomas
Rod Black
Ron Ellis
Ron Maclean
Rudy Giuliani
Sandra Post
Sandy Norton
Sarasota Technical Institution
Seven Keys to Happiness, Tee and Trish Ross
Shae-Lynn Bourne
Shania Twain, Canadian Country Music Awards
Shirley Soloman
Silken Laumann
Spencer Johnson, M.D., Peaks and Valleys
Sponsorship & Marketing, York University
Sponsorship Certification Program, George Brown of
Applied Arts
Stella Umeh
Stephen Covey
Steve Smith
Stress Solutions, Career Track
Susan Agulkark
Susan Gilmour
Susan Hay
Tamara Lowe
Team Dynamics
Tenille Dixon

The Artist's Way, Julia Cameron
The BIG Idea, Donny Deutsch
The Canadian Snowbird Guide, Douglas A. Gray
The Enneagram Institute
The Entrepreneur's Source, Scot Cummin
The Grandfather of Possibilities, Arlene Klein
The Mental Side of Golf, Charles M. Bonasera
The Psychology of Achievement, Brian Tracy
The Sacred Art of Listening, Brenda Ueland
Tie Domi
TiredofWaiting.com
Toastmasters International
Todd Brokker
Todd Stottlemyre
Tom Cheek
Tom Gibney
Tony Robbins
Toronto Blue Jays
Travel the World for Free, GO Global Publications
True Colors, Career Life Skills Resources Inc.
University of Toronto
USA The land of Opportunity
Warren Hudson
Wendel Clark
Who Moved My Cheese, Spencer Johnson, M.D.
Winning over Others
Winnipeg Transitions Centre
Young Entrepreneurs of Sarasota
Zig Ziglar

*Creativity*Guaranteed.com

I wish to express my gratitude to the following people for making my ride thrilling, safe & fun:

Adeola Joseph, my apprentice
Arnold Palmer, for loaning me his club
Art Linkletter, for inspiring
Bill Elam, for sharing
Carla Collins, my loyal and funny friend
Catherine Smith
Charles Bonasera, my mentor, friend and advisor
Diane Lane, my angelic friend
Diane Marlo, my very first coach
Dini Petty, for her confidence in me
Doctor Wayne Dyer, my inspiration
Doug Ross, PhD., my mentor and friend
Eric Lindros, for using his stardom for good
Fernando & Maria Alexander, living examples of the snowbird lifestyle
George Demarchi, for inspiring me
Georgia Brown & Dominick Medico, my mentors
Helen Mattar, my grammarian and editor
Helena Alexandre, my dear friend
Irene Vrbensky, my loyal friend and cheerleader
Jane & Dennis Blanchard, my Toastie friends
Jean Frances Touchbourne, for using our earth resources wisely
Jeanne Beker, Fashion Television
Jesse Millican, "come-back kid"
Joe Azari (Azzari), for investing in me

John Greer, jgas.us
Jon Burnside and the gang
John Meeks, my mentor and friend
Lady Patricia Dimitrou, my angel
Leonora & Stefano Girgenti, manifesters
Marie Osmond, for her honesty
Michael Briem, a dreamer who never gives up
Michele Holmes, for keeping me in one piece
Mike Nicota
Pierre Robitaille, who gave unconditionally
Rich & Rita Montemagno, for their trust
Richard Kiyosake, Rich Dad Poor Dad
Richard Lamb, teaching me how to drive a stick
Richard Roxborough, My Piano Man
Rick Senior, Deb, Rachel and Junior Haroutunian
Robert Demers, my first boss & dear friend
Robyn Abadie, my teacher and friend
Ron Klein, my book mentor and advisor
Rudy Giuliani for setting a superb example
Russell Starr, Picasso II
Ruth E Magee, World Traveler
Sandra Valente, my photo buddy
Shelley Aldred, for becoming a photographer
Stephen Renault, for my first professional break
Tee & Trish Ross, inspiring me to learn the piano
Tenille Dixon, Mary Kay consultant
Terry Mulligan, Mr. Optimism
Wendy Boyd, my first boss to give me creative
recognition and the freedom to express it

Finally, I wish to acknowledge
my Board of Advisors.
Although I am unable to name each of you
personally, I wish to express my infinite amount of
continued gratitude, respect, admiration and
sincere appreciation.

Tracey Parnell
CreativityGUARANTEED.com
The 40 Year Old Snowbird
Skype Facebook Linkedin
Photography Daniel Dutka, Toronto Photographer

February 14, 2010
CreativityGuaranteed.com
SnowBirdsofSarasota.ning.com

144

Board of Advisors

Clancey

Schnitzel

145

Schnapps

Angel

146

Zoee

Izzy and Ivan

Rex

147

*Creativity***Guaranteed**.com

Made in the USA
Lexington, KY
07 April 2015